BASEB

FORT WAYNE

Among the many great views within Memorial Stadium is the seating on the deck along the right field baseline. Fathers and sons, families, coworkers, or anyone seeking a unique place to obtain an intimate part of the game can find what they seek here. (Courtesy of the Fort Wayne Wizards.)

On the front cover: Please see page 44. (Courtesy of Don Graham.)
On the back cover: Please see page 28. (Courtesy of the Northeast Indiana Baseball Association.)
Cover background: Please see page 88. (Courtesy of the Fort Wayne Wizards.)

BASEBALL IN FORT WAYNE

Chad Gramling

ISBN 978-0-7385-4129-7

Published by Arcadia Publishing
Charleston, South Carolina

Printed in the United States of America

Library of Congress Catalog Card Number: 2006933971

For all general information contact Arcadia Publishing at:
Telephone 843-853-2070
Fax 843-853-0044
E-mail sales@arcadiapublishing.com
For customer service and orders:
Toll-Free 1-888-313-2665

Visit us on the Internet at www.arcadiapublishing.com

This book is dedicated to the men and women—past, present, and future—who have participated in Fort Wayne's baseball history as players, managers, coaches, sponsors, and supporters of the game. Without you, this book would not be possible.

CONTENTS

ACKNOWLEDGMENTS

Baseball in Fort Wayne is more than the title of a book. While I have made every effort to capture the history and passion for the game shared throughout the community, I have maintained a fear that I would be unable to properly chronicle the details with adequate justice.

Growing up in nearby Auburn, I was aware of the historical baseball significance in Fort Wayne. As an adult, I attended numerous Fort Wayne Wizards games with friends and family. But I had little idea about the decades in between. Many individuals and organizations helped to provide those details. Without that information, this book would be sorely incomplete.

Therefore I must thank many folks for their assistance. In no specific order, thank you to Jason Christopherson; Don Graham; Tim Kindler; Dick Crumback; Mike Nutter; Jim Shovlin; Robert Roethemeyer; Kelly Candaele; Andrew Bengs and the Fort Wayne Sports Corporation; Caleb Kimmel; Rob Bowen; Carolyn Spake-Leeper; Dana, Bob, and Joe at Office Concepts, Inc.; Tim Wiles at the National Baseball Hall of Fame; Donna Mclin; and all the players and team personnel who created the history so I could document it.

Specifically, I must also thank the Northeast Indiana Baseball Association and the Fort Wayne Wizards for their unbelievable support and willingness to assist in photographic collaboration.

Finally a special thank-you to my wife, Jenny, who has never discouraged any of my dreams—no matter how much baseball that has meant she must endure.

INTRODUCTION

Fort Wayne was among the first communities in the nation to embrace the game of baseball on a professional level. In 1862, a local group formed the Summit City Club. Over the next few years, additional teams formed, prompting local banking pioneer Allen Hamilton to donate land at the southwest corner of Lewis and Calhoun Streets to be used for organized baseball.

Following the Civil War, the team reunited to form the Fort Wayne Kekiongas in homage to Chief Little Turtle's settlement where the St. Joseph and St. Marys Rivers join to form the Maumee. In 1870, they prevailed as state champions. In March of the following year, the National Association of Professional Baseball Players (the National Association) formed.

The newly formed league was set to begin its inaugural year with the first contest between Boston and Washington, D. C., on May 3, 1871. However, rainfall postponed the game, opening the door for the Fort Wayne Kekiongas to host the Cleveland Forest Citys in the first organized professional baseball league contest the following day. The 2-0 victory pitched by the Kekiongas' Bobby Mathews saw the first shutout and first rain-shortened game, in addition to many other firsts, as was reported days later in the *New York Herald*:

> The finest game of base-ball ever witnessed in this country was played on the grounds of the Kekiongas, of this city, this afternoon—the playing throughout being without precedent in the annals of base-ball, the members of both clubs establishing beyond a doubt their reputation among the most skillful ball-players in the United States.

The team was made up of many locals and players recruited from a recently disbanded Baltimore club, through which the Kekiongas obtained opening day pitcher Bobby Mathews. Mathews went on to have a stellar professional career and is believed by many to be the inventor of the curveball.

Although the city had high hopes for the new venture—and even raced to build a playing field and grandstand so advanced for the era it was referred to as the "Grand Duchess"—enthusiasm soon waned in light of excessive losses, homesick Baltimore players leaving the team, and accusations of fixed contests.

Fort Wayne withdrew from the league in July with a 7-21 record and lagging local fan support. The Grand Duchess was destroyed by fire the following autumn. It is often contended that the team was sold to a Brooklyn club that later evolved to the present-day Los Angeles Dodgers. A more likely scenario, however, is that around the same time Fort Wayne withdrew from the league, the Brooklyn franchise paid their dues and sought acceptance to the league.

In 1883, a group of players united to form a team and enter the Northwestern League, which was the forerunner to today's American League. Fort Wayne remained a part of the league until 1891.

Also in 1883, the Jenney Electric Light Company provided 17 arc lamps so players could participate in what many have claimed to be the first lit night baseball game. It was certainly among the first night games, but others have also claimed rights to the same feat at earlier dates.

After stints in both major leagues, Fort Wayne embraced the emergence of minor-league ball. Following participation in the Tri-State League, Fort Wayne joined the Interstate Leagues and eventually spent many off-and-on-again seasons in the Central League.

In 1903, the Central League championship flag flew over League Park on Calhoun Street. The team won a second the following year before failing to renew its franchise for the 1905 season. From 1905 to 1907, the city enjoyed a successful semiprofessional stint.

In 1908, Claude Varnell moved the Springfield, Ohio, franchise of the Central League to Fort Wayne and, with the help of baseball promoter Martin Cleary, enticed Jack Hendricks to lead the team as manager. The team enjoyed much success: one pennant win (in 1912), three second-place finishes, two third, and one fourth. Additionally, many of the team's players would go on to take the field with major-league teams.

Varnell, who had hopes of one day owning a major-league team, sold the Fort Wayne squad in 1914, despondent that he could not turn a profit despite fielding winning teams. He returned to Wheeling, West Virginia, and died of pneumonia one year later at the age of 43.

In 1915, the Fort Wayne club finished last in a league of six teams despite a 63-59 record. After forgoing league play in 1916, Fort Wayne was again represented in league play in 1917, but again finished last. Fort Wayne did not have a representative in league play again until 1928, partly due to World War I.

In 1919, Martin Cleary played an integral role in fielding a semiprofessional team sponsored by Lincoln Life Insurance Company. Over the years, Cleary and his son, Bruff, were successful in bringing several major-league teams to League Park for exhibitions against the Lincoln Lifers squad. Teams such as the Philadelphia Athletics, New York Giants, Philadelphia Nationals, and Cincinnati Reds made stops in Fort Wayne during this period.

In 1923, the Indiana-Ohio League formed, consisting of Fort Wayne, Angola, Bryan, and Garrett. The following year, the Chiefs relocated under the guidance of C. L. Spence. The team easily took the Michigan-Indiana League crown that year but disbanded at Sturgis soon thereafter. The Lincoln Lifers resumed play in 1925 to fill the city's baseball void.

The year 1926 saw the return of the New York Giants in exhibition play. The next year, 1927 (the same year Babe Ruth hit 60 home runs), the Great Bambino slugged a 10th-inning blast in front of 3,000 spectators to break a 3-3 tie and send his team back to New York victorious. It was the final year of the Lifers

In 1928, Fort Wayne returned to the Central League with the newly formed Chiefs team and easily took the first half crown, largely due to the hitting exploits of Chuck Klein, who would go on to become one of the National League's all-time great hitters in Philadelphia.

The following year, the Chiefs became a farm team of the St. Louis Cardinals. However, the relationship lasted only one year following the Cardinals' decision to sever ties with the club. A local automobile dealer, Chet Schiefer, purchased the club and operated it independently.

In 1930, a new semiprofessional team picked up when the local division of the Pennsylvania Railroad fielded a team that eventually took the league crown in two consecutive seasons. During this same time, the local Federation League developed in 1931.

In 1934, the Chiefs launched to a seemingly insurmountable lead, prompting all other teams in the league to surrender the season. The following year, Fort Wayne joined the short-lived Three-I League, which consisted of teams from Indiana, Iowa, and Illinois. The team was led by former St. Louis Cardinals standout Bruno Betzel but suffered through a dismal season in what would be the last league play in the city until 1949.

During the absence of league play in the city, Edward "Red" Carrington became president of the amateur loop and generated significant interest in the Fort Wayne Federation League. It was an era characterized with outstanding play in the Federation League and teams who went on to win state, national, and global championships.

In 1948, while the semiprofessional GE Voltmen and the Fort Wayne Daisies of the All-American Girls Professional Baseball League (AAGPBL) were taking the field, Fort Wayne's reentry into the Central League (the Generals) created a crowded baseball climate in the city. The Generals lasted only one season.

The following year, the GE Voltmen returned home after winning a third consecutive championship. Despite the success, General Electric did not sponsor the team any longer, prompting the formation of the Fort Wayne Civic Baseball Association, with the intent of operating the semiprofessional team independently. It chose to call its team the Kekiongas to honor the city's first entry into organized professional baseball.

In 1950, staring financial hardship in the face, team management secured sponsorship from the Capehart-Farnsworth Company. The team, ably led by manager John "Red" Braden, took a fourth consecutive national championship.

Although there were no championships during the years immediately following, the semiprofessional club secured exhibition victories over the Washington Senators in 1951 as well as the St. Louis Browns and Chicago White Sox in 1953. In 1954, it fell to the Phillies and split an exhibition doubleheader with the Daisies.

In 1955, Allen Dairy assumed sponsorship of a team that lost only six games and was again led by Braden. The following year, the team took state and national crowns before capturing a second world semiprofessional title.

The Daisies' legacy was further documented and preserved in 1986 when Kelly Candaele, the son of former Fort Wayne Daisies star Helen Callaghan Candaele (St. Aubin), produced a documentary of an AAGPBL reunion that took place in Fort Wayne. After appearing on PBS, the film was later made into a feature film of the same title: *A League of Their Own*. Many of the film's roles were loosely based upon former Daisies players.

Beginning in the late 1950s and 1960s, the sport was mainly represented through the Fort Wayne Federation League as well as other industrial leagues. Often teams from other leagues would face each other in unofficial city championship games where bragging rights and an opportunity to excel on the field were the main prizes.

In 1992, word began to spread that professional baseball would be returning to Fort Wayne in the form of minor-league baseball. The Kenosha Twins, faced with struggling attendance and an antiquated stadium, announced they were relocating the team to Fort Wayne. The following year, the Fort Wayne Wizards took the field at Memorial Stadium for the first time.

The first season ticket was purchased by Braden, who had led the semiprofessional clubs to unprecedented championships and had long envisioned a day when professional baseball would return to Fort Wayne. On April 19, 1993, manager Jim Dwyer led the new club onto the field in front of 6,111 in attendance. Wizards pitcher Scott Moten threw the first pitch to Dan Madsen of visiting Peoria. Madsen and the next two batters struck out to provide the first three outs in Memorial Stadium history. Ramon Valette's two-run shot in the third inning helped lead the Wizards to a 7-2 victory.

Since that damp April evening, the Wizards have entertained and performed in front of hundreds of thousands of fans. During that span, the careers of many eventual Major League Baseball players have included stints in Fort Wayne.

Between 1993 and 2006, more than 50 former Fort Wayne Wizards have gone on to play at the major-league level. Additionally the Wizards have twice hosted major-league teams in exhibition play. The Castle has also fielded Major League Baseball tryouts, music concerts, and special appearances from local and national celebrities in addition to entertaining fans with on-field acts between innings.

As 2006 unfolded, talk of a new downtown stadium was a hot topic while discussing downtown enhancements in Fort Wayne. Drawing on examples from other minor-league baseball cities, a recommendation for the development of a new downtown stadium was made. As of this writing, nothing was definitive, but the prospects for a bright future for professional baseball in the city were very real.

The Fort Wayne Wizards have managed to overcome one of the primary hurdles that crippled many of the earlier ventures into professional baseball in Fort Wayne by generating a solid fan base to support the team. Having been named the Midwest League Team of the Year twice over the last four years, the Wizards have helped Fort Wayne attain the status of seventh-best minor-league market (of 230) in the country by *Street & Smith Sports Business Journal*. Under new ownership, a solid and growing fan base, unparalleled community outreach, and outstanding team leadership, the Fort Wayne Wizards look to continue their successful track record and add to the successes that have been the hallmark of their contributions to Fort Wayne baseball history. At the same time, the Fort Wayne Baseball Federation continues to provide a quality baseball experience within the local community, and the Northeast Indiana Baseball Association (NEIBA) offers a forum for preserving and honoring local contributions to the game.

Without a doubt, the spirit of America's national pastime is alive and well within Fort Wayne and northeast Indiana.

The Early Years

The game of baseball began in Fort Wayne years before the North and South took to the battlefields of the Civil War. Shortly after that war, the Kekiongas participated in the first organized professional baseball game. Despite the shortcomings of that season, it cemented the city's place in the history of America's national pastime. Photographs of that team, given its brief history, are extremely rare. Just as scarce are photographs of the fields and parks in which the team played. Unfortunately the life span of the Grand Duchess was only a few months longer than the team's. Fire totally engulfed the field just months after the team withdrew from the league. It was a total loss. Availability of photographs relating to baseball in Fort Wayne begins to increase in the era beginning with the early 1900s. Fortunately many of the city's greats who went on to play at the major-league level were immortalized through photograph syndication services, such as the Bain Syndicate. The photographs in this chapter relate to baseball in and about Fort Wayne during an early era of the sport, 1871 to 1930.

Several players transition between innings during a game taking place at the League Municipal Park. The historical park was later renamed Carrington Field in honor of local baseball ambassador Edward "Red" Carrington. When the Kenosha Twins relocated to Fort Wayne, Memorial Stadium was built in its place. At that time, Carrington Field was relocated across Coliseum Boulevard. (Courtesy of the Allen County Public Library.)

A 1914 postcard displays the field and grandstand used by the Fort Wayne Railroaders, which was the name of the city's Central League entry at the time. The team featured pitcher Jesse Haines, who would later win three World Series titles with the St. Louis Cardinals and be elected to the National Baseball Hall of Fame in 1970. (Courtesy of the Allen County Public Library.)

In what is probably a local high school team, several Fort Wayne players pose for this photograph. Although none of the players are identified, the man seated at the far right of the middle row appears to be longtime Fort Wayne baseball magnate Red Carrington. (Courtesy of the Northeast Indiana Baseball Association.)

The Concordia Walther League team of Fort Wayne (around 1925) features Lou Holterman (standing at far right), who was first baseman and player-manager. Following the organization of the Fort Wayne Oldtimers Baseball Association (later to evolve into the Northeast Indiana Baseball Association [NEIBA]), Holterman was elected to be the first inductee of the local hall of fame. (Courtesy of the Northeast Indiana Baseball Association.)

The Fort Wayne Baseball Club of the Central League poses for a team photograph to commemorate the 1913 season. From left to right are (first row) ? O'Mara, ? Dennis (secretary), team president Claude Varnell, ? Burke (manager), and ? Martin; (second row) ? Ainsworth and ? Wagner; (third row) ? Bratchie, ? Welsh, ? Nespo, ? Atkins, ? Anderson, ? Loudermilk, ? Tauman, ? Young, and ? Colligan. Varnell, who owned the team, hoped to gain enough experience to own a major-league team, spending much of his own money in doing so. Despite fielding winning clubs and being among the most prominent baseball men of the Central League, Varnell was never able to produce equal success at the gates. He sold the team to Central League president Louis C. Heilbroner and a contingent of local stockholders and died a short time later after suffering from pneumonia. (Author's collection.)

Posing here are unidentified players and team representatives of the local Benevolent and Protective Order of Elks entry. The time frame in which this photograph was taken is around 1900. The man standing in the back row, second from the left, may be Louis C. Heilbroner, who was a highly visible and well-known Fort Wayne baseball representative of his day. (Courtesy of the Northeast Indiana Baseball Association.)

This unidentified Fort Wayne squad is featured in a fascinating photograph that is located in the NEIBA Museum. No player names or dates accompany the photograph, but judging by the grandstand in the background of the photograph, it is assumed to be one of the early Central League entries. (Courtesy of the Northeast Indiana Baseball Association.)

Maxmillian George Carnarius was a Terre Haute native and the son of Prussian immigrants. At age 13, his father enrolled him at Concordia College in Fort Wayne. After graduating in 1909, he enrolled in Concordia Seminary in St. Louis. That summer, he attended a Central League game in Terre Haute and convinced the South Bend manager to fill the team's shortstop vacancy with him the next day. He remained in the lineup the remainder of the season. To preserve his amateur status, his name was recorded as "Max Carey," and he went by it the rest of his life. The Pittsburgh Pirates purchased Carey near the conclusion of the 1910 season, and he remained with the club for nearly two decades, retiring after the 1929 season to cap a hall of fame career with 2,665 hits, 738 stolen bases, and a .285 lifetime average. In 1944, he was hired to manage in the All-American Girls Professional Baseball League (AAGPBL). After winning the pennant that season, he served as the league's president through 1950. (Courtesy of the Library of Congress, Prints and Photographs Division, LC-B2-4998-3.)

Bill Wambsganns played 13 major-league seasons. However, he is most known for executing the only unassisted triple play in World Series history, which occurred during the 1920 World Series. During the fifth inning of Game 5, there were runners on first and second. A sharp liner was hit to Wambsganns, who caught it, stepped on second base and tagged the Brooklyn runner coming from first. Wambsganns's father was a Lutheran minister who transferred from Cleveland to Fort Wayne. For a short time, Wambsganns began to follow in his father's footsteps by enrolling at Concordia College in Fort Wayne but decided to become a professional baseball player instead. He was downgraded to minor-league duty after the 1926 season and retired as a player in 1932. Wambsganns later returned to Fort Wayne, where he managed the Fort Wayne Daisies. (Courtesy of the Library of Congress, Prints and Photographs Division, LC-B2-5550-19.)

Bruno Betzel played five seasons with the St. Louis Cardinals from 1914 to 1918. After his playing days ended, Betzel managed in Fort Wayne for one season. He is shown here as a member of the Cardinals. (Courtesy of the Library of Congress, Prints and Photographs Division, LC-B2-3579-12.)

Hailing from New Haven, Indiana, brothers William "Pinky" Hargrave (left) and Eugene Franklin "Bubbles" Hargrave both enjoyed lengthy careers in Major League Baseball. At the time this photograph was taken in 1930, Pinky was with the Detroit Tigers, and Bubbles was a member of the New York Yankees. While they were not the first set of brothers to play catcher at the major-league level, they are one of only 14 known. (Courtesy of the Northeast Indiana Baseball Association.)

Pinky Hargrave poses on the steps of a dugout while he was a member of the Washington Senators. While he did not post quite the same type of offensive numbers that his brother did, his defensive skills kept him in the big leagues for many years. Interestingly, Hargrave batted right-handed in his first four seasons and then became a switch-hitter in 1928. From 1933 on, he batted only left-handed. His nickname was said to have been the result of his flaming red hair. Hargrave was elected to the Northeast Indiana Baseball Hall of Fame in 1964. (Courtesy of the Library of Congress, Prints and Photographs Division, LC-B2-6252-14.)

Bubbles Hargrave practices his batting form in this photograph taken while he was a member of the Cincinnati Reds. He was elected to the Northeast Indiana Baseball Hall of Fame in 1962. (Courtesy of the Library of Congress, Prints and Photographs Division, LC-B2-3172-1.)

Eugene Franklin Hargrave is said to have received the nickname of Bubbles because he would stutter when saying words that began with the letter *b*. However, Bubbles Hargrave was a catcher best remembered for being one of only two catchers to win the National League batting title in 1926. At the time, league rules stipulated a player must appear in at least 100 games to qualify for consideration. While he did not catch in that many games, he took on a pinch-hitter role at times, which enabled him to qualify. (Courtesy of the Library of Congress, Prints and Photographs Division, LC-B2-6034-9 [above] and LC-B2-3172-2 [below].)

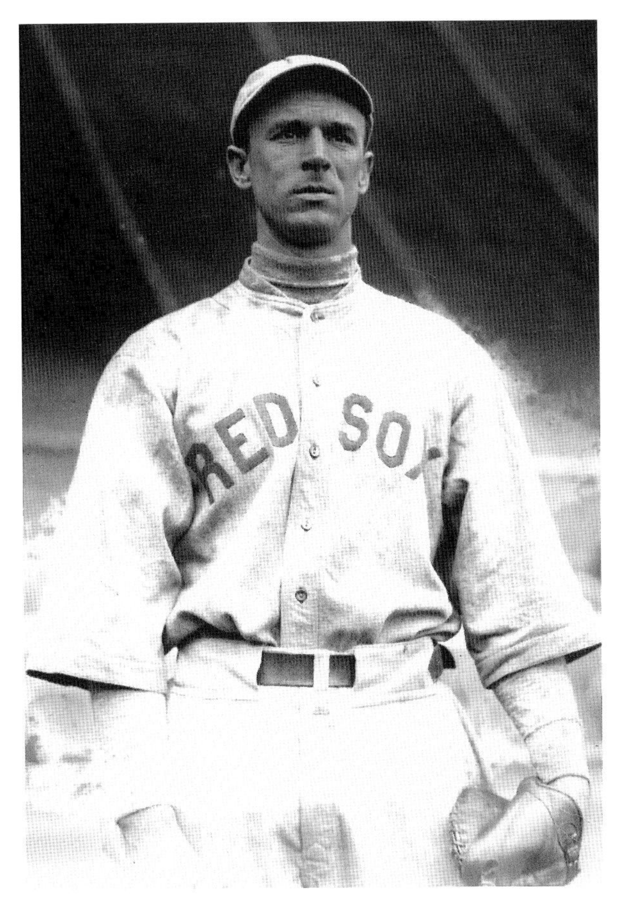

First baseman Del Gainer (pictured in both pictures on the page) entered professional baseball in 1909 with a club in Grafton, West Virginia. He later spent a year in the Central League with Fort Wayne and was sent up to the Detroit Tigers in 1911, only to be returned to Fort Wayne a short while later for additional development. Detroit sold Gainer to Boston after he sat out the better part of the 1912 season due to a broken wrist. When World War I began, Gainer left the game to serve in the U.S. Navy, after which he rejoined the Red Sox in 1915 where he took on a utility player role on the world championship team. Also on that team was another player with Fort Wayne ties, Everett Scott. (Courtesy of the Library of Congress, Prints and Photographs Division, LC-B2-3637-12 [above] and LC-B2-3962-12 [below].)

An Auburn, Indiana, native, Rollie Zeider is one of only a few players who played with three different major Chicago clubs (Cubs, White Sox, and Chi-Feds/Whales). He is also a member of an even more exclusive club—players who have played in three major leagues, the National League, the American League, and the Federal League. Zeider was well known as a fast base runner, swiping 49 in his rookie season with the White Sox, a record that stood for 76 years. After his big-league days ended, he played the 1919 season with the Toledo Mudhens. When he finally stopped playing professionally, he ran a restaurant called Polly's Tavern in Garrett, Indiana, and was elected to the Northeast Indiana Baseball Hall of Fame in 1962. Shown here, Zeider displays his hitting and fielding skills for the camera. (Courtesy of the Library of Congress, Prints and Photographs Division, LC-B2-2451-3 [above] and LC-B2-4621-4 [below].)

The Fort Wayne Shamrocks were organized in 1897 and remained active through 1918. They were considered to be one of the most well-known semiprofessional teams in the middle states. During their history, many men of the team went on to play at the major-league level, and they played primarily as an independent team. Pictured from left to right are (top row) ? Gage, Charlie Koons, J. C. Smith, and ? Centlivre; (second row) W. Y. Cherry, manager Martin Cleary, and Fred "Cyclone" Alberts; (third row) George Nill, ? Longfield, ? Walda, and H. A. Ehle; (fourth row) ? Erickson, ? Beach, ? Hoffer, and ? Robbins. Martin Cleary managed and scouted talent for the Shamrocks from the team's beginning in 1897 through his resignation in November 1913. Of the group pictured, Alberts, Beach, Koons, and Nill are members of the NEIBA Hall of Fame. (Courtesy of Tim Kindler.)

Everett Scott once held the title of baseball's "ironman." Shown here, Scott poses for a profile shot (above) and playfully fields during pregame activities (below). A Bluffton, Indiana, native, Scott broke into Major League Baseball with the Boston Red Sox in 1914 and enjoyed a successful 13-year career, also playing with the Yankees, Senators, White Sox, Cubs, and Orioles. Nicknamed the "Deacon," Scott played on six World Series teams. His consecutive game streak of 1,307 began on June 20, 1916, and concluded on May 6, 1916, the same year his teammate Lou Gehrig began his consecutive game streak of 2,130 games. (Courtesy of the Library of Congress, Prints and Photographs Division, LC-B2-989-15 [above] and LC-B2-992-4 [below].)

Edward Pfeffer, who went by Jeff, joined the Fort Wayne Central League club in 1910. After winning 29 games during two seasons, his contract was purchased by the St. Louis Browns. Following just 10 innings of relief, the team released him back to the Central League, where he played for Grand Rapids after a stint with a Denver club. Nicknamed "Big Jeff," he later led the 1916 Dodgers to a pennant with 25 wins. In 1921, the Dodgers traded him to the Cardinals where he won 19 games the following season. Pfeffer finished his major-league career with 158 wins, including 28 shutouts, 194 complete games, and a 3.13 ERA. (Courtesy of the Library of Congress, Prints and Photographs Division, LC-B2-3936-13.)

The Lady Wayne Chocolates sponsored a baseball team in Fort Wayne in the late 1920s and early 1930s. Shown here is Lou Holterman, the first inductee of the Northeast Indiana Baseball Hall of Fame. Holterman played with the Lady Wayne Chocolates club from 1929 to 1931. (Courtesy of Don Graham.)

At age 26, Ray Pepper broke into the big leagues in April 1932 with the St. Louis Cardinals. He played until 1936, finishing his career with the St. Louis Browns over three seasons. Shown in this picture is Pepper as a member of the 1929 Fort Wayne Chiefs. (Courtesy of the Northeast Indiana Baseball Association.)

The author speculates this squad, consisting of players from multiple local teams, is an all-star team. No players are identified; however, the photograph was taken sometime in the 1930s. (Author's collection.)

THE LEGACY CONTINUES

Into the 1930s and 1940s, Fort Wayne's participation in the Central League loop waned. In its place, the Fort Wayne Federation League took center stage on local ball diamonds. During this era, baseball flourished under the direction of figureheads like Red Carrington, Bob Parker, and John "Red" Braden in addition to the contributions of countless players, managers, and sponsors who made the game an essential form of entertainment in the Summit City. In the late 1940s and early 1950s, the Federation League shared the spotlight with the girls of summer when the Fort Wayne Daisies of the AAGPBL moved into the city. With three options for local fans to take in baseball games, it was a crowded—yet exciting—baseball environment. This era also represents an initiative to formally organize a body of individuals who would be responsible for maintaining and preserving the game's heritage within the city. The establishment of the entity that would eventually evolve to the current NEIBA and accompanying hall of fame occurred and continues to support that legacy to this day.

Believed to have been taken in the 1930s or 1940s, an unidentified Fort Wayne City Lights team poses for a photograph in front of an elaborate stacking of baseball bats. This photograph was used as the background for the cover of the book. (Courtesy of the Northeast Indiana Baseball Association.)

An early City Lights team poses for a group photograph. From left to right are (first row) Norbert Hohman, Vic Ruby, Carl Schoenle, and unidentified; (second row) Glen Wolfcale, Wayne Scott, Howard Korn, Paul Straight, John Ramp, Zulu Bolyard, "Monk" Wilson, and Al Schoenle. (Courtesy of the Northeast Indiana Baseball Association.)

The 1948 Fort Wayne Generals of the Central League take time out from practice to pose for a team photograph. Although most of the players in the photograph are unidentified, those that are include; ? Cuttitta (third row, second from left), ? Beck (third row, third from left), ? Gabrieli (third row, second from right), ? Schuster (second row, second from left), and ? Corridan (first row, second from right). (Courtesy of the Northeast Indiana Baseball Association.)

A group of local ballplayers of a team calling itself the Independents poses for a team photograph along the third-base line of the field. Large billboard signs appear in the background, as does the scoreboard on the right side of the photograph. (Courtesy of the Northeast Indiana Baseball Association.)

Shown in this undated photograph are many representatives of the Fort Wayne Baseball Federation, taken at an unidentified park. Particularly interesting about this photograph is the variety of local jerseys that appear on the players who are in the group. (Courtesy of the Northeast Indiana Baseball Association.)

Shown here, an unidentified group of individuals sits on a section of bleachers at a Fort Wayne area baseball park for a photograph. Most jerseys in the group are the same, leading the author to conclude the photograph is a team photograph. (Courtesy of the Northeast Indiana Baseball Association.)

Several players appear in a group photograph in what is most likely a mixture of junior and senior division players from the Fort Wayne Baseball Federation League. Shown in the middle row are two players wearing City Lights jerseys. (Courtesy of the Northeast Indiana Baseball Association.)

Shown here is a photograph of an early local entry of the General Electric baseball team. No player identifications are available, but the photograph is believed to have been taken sometime around 1923. (Courtesy of Don Graham)

The 1948 General Electric (GE Voltmen) club would go on to become national semiprofessional champions. Shown from left to right are (first row) coach Dee Hamilton, Bill Brandt, Paul Dyke, John Corridan, and manager John "Red" Braden; (second row) Bob Winters, Stan Shargey, Pete Elko, Truett "Rip" Sewell, Bill Hardy, and batboy Jimmy Slack; (third row) Al Hazle, Olan Smith, Charlie Harmon, Rudy Rundus, Art Gabrielli, Hugh Orphan, and Charlie Shipman. (Courtesy of Don Graham.)

In an undated photograph of the General Electric club, the team poses for a photograph. It is likely that this team is of the 1949 season or later. (Courtesy of the Northeast Indiana Baseball Association.)

Although none of the player identifications could be confirmed, this image represents the City Lights Tigers and is believed to be taken around 1935 at Pennsy Park, which was located on South Anthony Boulevard just south of Wayne Trace. Standing at the far left is Federation League president O. L. Fawley, and standing at the far right is league secretary Red Carrington. The City Lights team won the city's first state championship in 1931. (Courtesy of the Northeast Indiana Baseball Association.)

Winning the playoff from the St. Joe squad, the Heco-Eskay nine earned the right to represent the Fort Wayne Baseball Federation in the 1934 National Amateur Baseball Federation tournament in Youngstown, Ohio. Pictured from left to right are (first row) Russ DeTurk, Paul Fair, "Rirpo" Steinhauser, mascot Robert Reeder, Ted Bohnke, John Forney, and Arn Benecke; (second row) manager Harold Scherer, "Chuch" Bobilya, Elmer Gebhard, George Langenberg, league secretary Red Carrington, Ralph Troyer, Bill Johnston, Ed Bornkamp, and league president O. L. Fawley. The Fort Wayne squad was eliminated after being defeated in its first two contests of the tournament. (Courtesy of the Northeast Indiana Baseball Association.)

The Smith Coalers (above) defeated the Tod-Centlivre team (below) to earn the right to represent the Fort Wayne Federation League in the 1935 National Amateur Baseball Federation tournament in Cleveland. Shown above, from left to right, are (first row) ? Maxfield, ? Van Zile, ? Miller, ? Strader, and H. Kreigh; (second row) manager and sponsor Harry Smith, league secretary Red Carrington, ? Snyder, ? Springer, ? Smith, ? Meyers, ? Karuss, ? Sterline, league president O. L. Fawley, mascot ? Branning. The Coalers were ousted from their tournament after posting a 1-2 record, their victory coming in Game 2 against Indianapolis. For the Tod-Centlivre team, shown in the bottom picture, from left to right are (first row) mascot Robert Reeder; (second row) ? Krause, ? Bobilya, ? Langerberg, ? Troyer, ? Nahrwaold, ? Slater, Louis "Jap" Voirol, and ? Ellenwood; (third row) sponsor Tod Soliday, Red Carrington, ? Lakey, ? Himmelstein, ? Steiny, ? Kohnke, ? Cartwright, ? Harber, manager ? Forney, and O. L. Fawley. (Courtesy of the Northeast Indiana Baseball Association.)

In an undated photograph with unidentified players, the team appears to contain at least portions of the General Electric club at the time as evidenced by the players in the far left of the back row and the far right of the front row. (Courtesy of the Northeast Indiana Baseball Association.)

Centlivre Beer was a frequent sponsor of Fort Wayne Federation League baseball teams in the 1930s. Shown is one of the teams the company sponsored. With the exception of league secretary Red Carrington (show in the back row on the far right), none of the players are identified. (Courtesy of the Northeast Indiana Baseball Association.)

Tod's Place was another frequent sponsor of Fort Wayne Federation League baseball teams. No dates or player identifications are available for this photograph. League secretary Red Carrington is standing in the back row, fifth from the left. (Courtesy of the Northeast Indiana Baseball Association.)

Having won the right to represent Fort Wayne in the meet, the Tod-Centlivre baseball squad prepared for the 1936 National Amateur Baseball Federation tournament in Cleveland. Pictured above, from left to right, are (first row) mascot Robert Reeder; (second row) ? Baker, ? Moore, Louis "Jap" Voirol, ? Langenberg, ? Troyer, ? Berwert, ? Bobilya, and P. Bolyard; (third row) league president O. L. Fawley, ? Meyers, ? Lombardo, ? Harber, ? Slater, team sponsor Tod Soliday, ? Kraus, ? Ellenwood, ? Huimmelstein, manager ? Forney, and league secretary Red Carrington. Despite reaching the semifinals, the Detroit and Dayton squads overpowered the locals 6-0 and 9-1, respectively. (Courtesy of the Northeast Indiana Baseball Association.)

The Superior Malt-Berghoff squad finished in first place in the Fort Wayne Federation League and won the postseason tournament to earn the right to represent Fort Wayne in the 1937 National Amateur Baseball Federation tournament, which took place in Dayton. From left to right are (first row) mascot Bill Weber Jr.; (second row) ? Fox, ? Slater, ? Krauss, ? Kramer, ? Leichty, ? Stauffer, and ? Miller; (third row) league secretary Red Carrington, ? Farrell, ? Van Skyock, ? Cowan, Louis "Jap" Voirol, ? Binger, ? Doehrman, ? Kestner, manager Bill Weber, and league president O. L. Fawley. (Courtesy of the Northeast Indiana Baseball Association.)

Shown in this photograph is the Fort Wayne Federation League Veterans of Foreign Wars (VFW) Post No. 857 entry in 1940. The team was the last to win a championship in the Fort Wayne Baseball Federation at old Pennsy Park. Most members of the team were in their last season with the federation and were players on the first championship team, the City Light Tigers. From left to right are (first row) Jack Fox, Bob Bolyard, Vic Ruby, manager Jim Baker, batboy Jim Davis, Adam Farrell, Howard Pense, and Curly Armstrong; (second row) league secretary-treasurer Elmer Wagner, Al Schoenle, Johnny Ramp, Herb Strombeck, Zulu Bolyard, Cocky Roberts, Ozzie Bolyard, coach Ross Aikens, business manager and VFW representative Chick Fenton, and league president Red Carrington. (Courtesy of the Northeast Indiana Baseball Association.)

Fort Wayne Federation League secretary Red Carrington presents an MVP award to Tod's Place standout "Fuzz" Himmelstein during the 1930s. (Courtesy of the Northeast Indiana Baseball Association.)

Louis "Jap" Voirol, hurler of the Superior Malt-Berghoff club, is awarded an MVP trophy in the Fort Wayne Federation League by Red Carrington. The award was presented just prior to game time; after that, he went to the mound and was defeated by the Tod-Nickel-Plates team. Voirol achieved a 7-2 record during the regular season, his third year in the league. (Courtesy of the Northeast Indiana Baseball Association.)

Proving that baseball is not solely a man's sport in Fort Wayne, several women (possibly wives or girlfriends of Federation League players at the time) show their affection for the game by each taking a hand on the bat. (Courtesy of the Northeast Indiana Baseball Association.)

The Fort Wayne Daisies entered the AAGPBL in 1952 and were a successful franchise despite never clearing the last hurdle to win a championship (they came close several times). Shown here are five Daisies rookies. From left to right are unidentified, Arleen Johnson Noga, Penny O'Brien Cooke, Yolande Teillet, and Irene Rhunke Saranlas. (Courtesy of Don Graham.)

The 1949 Fort Wayne Daisies, shown from left to right, are (first row) Wilma Briggs, Betty Petryna, Thelma "Tiby" Eisen, Donna Cook, Nancy Mudge, and Jean Smith; (second row) Ruby Heafner, Betty Luna, Vivian "Viv" Kellogg, Kay Blumetta, and Maxine Kline; (third row) Mary Roundtree, Marge Pepper, Dottie Schroeder, chaperone Gerry Reiber, manager Harold Greiner, Millie Deegan, June Pappas, and Evelyn "Evie" Wawryshyn. (Courtesy of Don Graham.)

The 1951 Fort Wayne Daisies team poses for a team photograph in front of the scoreboard. Shown from left to right are (first row) Mirta Marrero, unidentified, Thelma "Tiby" Eisen, Evelyn "Evie" Wawryshn, unidentified, Mary Roundtree, and Isabel Alvarez; (second row) Doris Tetzlaf, Katie Horstman, Jean Geisinger, Pat Scott, manager Max Carey, Katie Vonderau, Wilma Briggs, and Lois Young; (third row) Dottie Schroeder, Maxine Kline, Betty Weaver Foss, Fran Janssen, Jo Weaver, Millie Deegan, and Jean Weaver. (Courtesy of Don Graham.)

Helen Callaghan Candaele (St. Aubin), the left-handed Daisies outfielder, was sometimes called "the Ted Williams of Women's Baseball." In her career year of 1945, she tied for the league lead in home runs, led in total bases with 156, and was second in steals with 92, first in hits with 122, and second in runs with 77. She also was first in doubles with 17. Of her four children, her son Casey followed in her footsteps and played professionally. Another son, Kelly, produced the 1986 documentary *A League of Their Own*, which focuses on an AAGPBL reunion that took place in Fort Wayne. It later became the inspiration for the motion picture of the same name. (Courtesy of Don Graham.)

Lilian "Lil" Jackson participated in the AAGPBL from 1943 to 1945 as a member of the Fort Wayne Daisies, Rockford Peaches, and Minneapolis Milleretes. Shown here, she connects on a pitch before heading to first. (Courtesy of the Northeast Indiana Baseball Association.)

Vivian "Viv" Kellogg joined the Minneapolis Millerettes in the spring of 1944. She began the 1945 season with the Fort Wayne Daisies, who had replaced the Millerettes, and continued to play first base there until injuries forced her to retire in 1950. In 1988, Kellogg was recognized with other women of the AAGPBL by the National Baseball Hall of Fame. In 2002, she was inducted into the NEIBA Hall of Fame. (Courtesy of Don Graham.)

Marge Callaghan (Maxwell) was the older sister of Daisies teammate Helen Callaghan. She broke into the league with the Minneapolis Millerettes and joined the Daisies when the team relocated in 1945. She was elected to the Canadian Baseball Hall of Fame alongside her sister in June 1998. (Courtesy of Don Graham.)

Following the disbanding of the AAGPBL, several women organized the All-American "All Girl" Baseball Team to tour and continue their role in the sport. Pictured in the photograph (about 1955–1957) are former Fort Wayne Daisies Jean Geisinger (first row, second from right), Maxine Kline, Jo Weaver, Katie Horstman, Dottie Schroeder, and manager Bill Allington (far right). Having managed his teams to titles in 1945, 1948, and 1949, Allington won more games than any other manager in AAGPBL history. (Courtesy of Don Graham.)

The 1956 Allen Dairy team prevailed as Global World Series champions by beating out all competition during a tournament held in Milwaukee. Shown from left to right are (first row) Walt Wherry, Ed Wopinek, Jim Mason, manager John "Red" Braden, Charles Huwer, and Dean Wood; (second row) Jim La Marque, Parnel Hisner, Olan Smith, Wilmer Fields, Pete Olsen, Don Pavletich, John Kennedy, and Pete Stamen. In the foreground are several trophies earned by the team throughout the tournament. From left to right are Best Defensive Team, Leading Hitter (Olan Smith), Team Championship Trophy, Outstanding Outfielder (Charles Huwer), Leading Pitcher (Pete Olsen), and Individual Sportsmanship (John Braden). (Courtesy of Don Graham.)

The Fort Wayne Capeharts semiprofessional team accepts its trophy after winning the National Semi-Pro Championship. John "Red" Braden (center) is all smiles as he holds the award for the photograph. Other Capeharts players standing, in no specific order, are Charlie Shipman, Dee Hamilton, Sal SS Madrid, Maynard Dewitt, and Hershel Held. The trophy is now on display at the NEIBA Museum. (Courtesy of Don Graham.)

Fort Wayne's John Kennedy slides into home plate during a United States and Hawaii game played during the Global World Series. The catcher is Hawaii's Sal Recca, and the umpire is Chief Meyer. Kennedy's teammate Olan Smith stays clear of the play. The Fort Wayne Allen Dairymen went on to win the game 5-3 and would go on to become the tournament champions for the second consecutive year. This photograph appears on the front cover of the book. (Courtesy of Don Graham.)

Teams representing eight nations of the world are introduced to fans in attendance before the opening games of the 1956 Global World Series at Milwaukee County Stadium. Clockwise from home plate are Japan, Puerto Rico, Hawaii, Canada, Columbia, Holland, United States (Fort Wayne Allen Dairymen), and Mexico. Fort Wayne returned home as global champions by outlasting all other teams in the tournament. (Courtesy of Don Graham.)

Shown in this photograph is batter Sharvey of the Capeharts, at the plate with the bases full in the eighth inning of the opening game against All-Kanebo in Japan during the 1950 Global World Series. Particularly interesting in this photograph is the signage in the outfield and the attire of the spectators seated along the first-base line. (Courtesy of Don Graham.)

Shown here is a junior entry to the Fort Wayne Federation League. Unfortunately none of the players are identified, and no date is available. (Courtesy of the Northeast Indiana Baseball Association.)

After he retired from baseball, Everett Scott returned to Fort Wayne and opened a bowling alley. It was located on South Calhoun Street, south of Lewis Street. It was on the second floor of a building that also housed the popular Sappenfield's Sports Shop. Those who worked for Scott as pin setters were paid by the game plus any tips paid by bowlers, which came in the form of change thrown down the alley after the games concluded. Pictured here, a much younger Everett Scott poses for a photograph while a member of the Boston Red Sox. (Courtesy of the Library of Congress, Prints and Photographs Division, LC-B2-3637-14.)

John "Red" Braden was an outstanding figure in Fort Wayne baseball for many years. As a player-manager, he led several semiprofessional teams, two of them to global world championships and others to national and state championships. On six occasions, he led his teams to wins over professional major-league teams during exhibition play. In 1965, he was elected to the NEIBA Hall of Fame, alongside former big-leaguers Rollie Zeider and Charles "Chick" Stahl (who was inducted posthumously having committed suicide many years before). In 1993, at the age of 82, Braden became the first season ticket holder in Fort Wayne Wizards history, seemingly linking Fort Wayne's baseball past to baseball present and future. (Courtesy of the Northeast Indiana Baseball Association.)

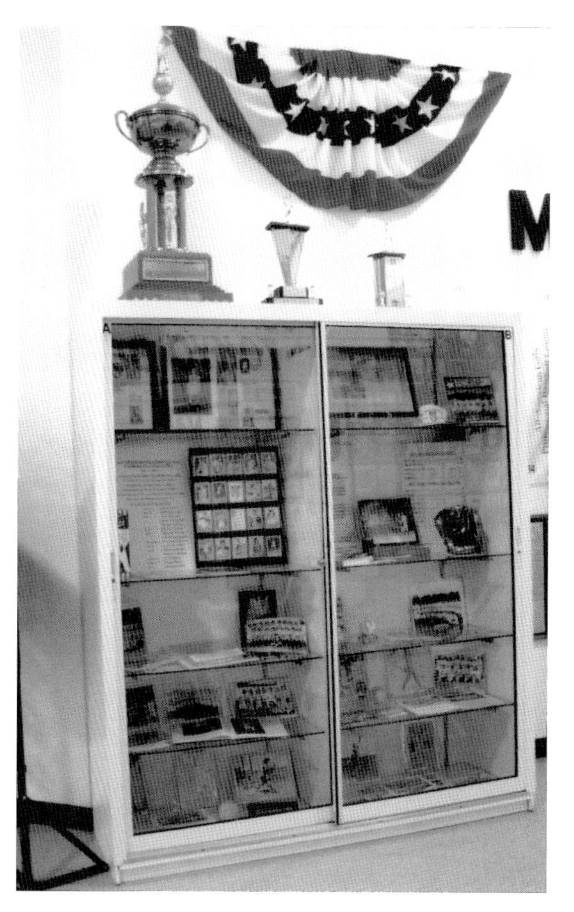

In 1946, several former baseball players banded together to informally sponsor actions to advance the sport on a local level. They became more organized over the following years and became a locally chartered branch of the National Hot Stove League of America in 1953. In 1961, the group again reorganized under a new name, the Fort Wayne Oldtimers Baseball Association and announced the development of a local hall of fame. In 1992, the name was changed to the Northeast Indiana Baseball Association (NEIBA) to reflect the group's endeavors and membership base. In 2002, a longtime goal of finding a permanent facility for the hall of fame and accompanying museum was realized. Shown here are photographs of the NEIBA Museum inside the Dean Kruse World War II Victory Museum in Auburn. The photograph below shows the 8-inch-by-10-inch photograph of each inducted hall of famer as they overlook the exhibits. (Author's collection.)

Amazing Baseball

In the early 1990s, word started to spread that the city of Fort Wayne would be getting a minor-league baseball team. The ownership group of the Kenosha Twins sought a new market where its team could flourish. Fort Wayne was selected, and the prospect of professional baseball in Fort Wayne quickly energized residents and businesses throughout the area. One of the initial and biggest questions asked in preparation for welcoming the club was where the team's home field would be located. The site of what was then Carrington Field was ultimately chosen to house the new Memorial Stadium—affectionately referred to as the Castle. Carrington Field was relocated across Coliseum Boulevard, and the two baseball entities enjoyed more than 13 years of concurrent baseball play (the Snider High School baseball team also played at Carrington Field during this time span). The first Fort Wayne Wizards game took place on April 19, 1993. More than 6,000 fans packed the Castle on a chilly, damp evening. Since that night, the Fort Wayne Wizards have enjoyed a long tenure within the city and have seen many of their players achieve success at the major-league level. In addition to providing an opportunity for the local citizenry to get a glimpse of exceptional play on the diamond, the organization has been a great community partner and supporter. The team's role has been a significant contributor in making Fort Wayne one of the best minor-league sports markets in the country.

Memorial Stadium was constructed on the site of former Carrington Field to be the home of the Fort Wayne Wizards minor-league baseball team. This photograph is clearly an early depiction of the Castle, evident by the lack of the now standing picnic and family areas behind right field, as well as the deck along the first-base line. In 1997, the field dimensions were 335 feet in left, 405 in center, and 335 in right. In 1999, both right and center fields were brought in 5 feet. (Courtesy of the Fort Wayne Wizards.)

Wizards fans pack the Castle during the early years, as evidenced by the lettering below the broadcast area, which was modified to the current lettering style prior to the 1999 season when the Wizards switched parent club affiliations from the Minnesota Twins to the San Diego Padres. Seating capacity at the Castle is 6,516. (Courtesy of the Fort Wayne Wizards.)

Shown here are two Fort Wayne Wizards team photographs. Both are undated but are definitely taken more recently as evidenced by the uniform styles and logos. The photograph above was taken in the center field area of Memorial Stadium. The photograph below was taken in front of home plate. The area above the team features the Fort Wayne Wizards name and bears the likeness of Dinger the Dragon, the team's mascot. During the tenure of the team's original ownership group, Dinger did not exist. Instead the team name was printed in a more Gothic style of print and bore the image of the team's original mascot, Wayne the Wizard, holding his palms over a crystal ball. (Courtesy of the Fort Wayne Wizards.)

The Wizards' early uniforms were gray with black lettering and included a black cap showing the letters *FW*. They are on display here as the team walks from the field following a game. Shown in the background are many billboardlike signs purchased by local and national sponsoring organizations. Such signage, done in a style that is reminiscent of traditional minor-league advertising, has been a mainstay at the Castle since the first year. Beyond the wall is Coliseum Boulevard. Netting is in place to prevent home run balls from making their way onto the busy street. (Courtesy of the Fort Wayne Wizards.)

Wayne the Wizard was the team's first mascot. Wayne would frequently walk among the fans in attendance during the game and on the concourse before the first pitch. He is shown here signing a ball cap and other items for excited young fans, with which he was always a hit. (Courtesy of the Fort Wayne Wizards.)

Quite slimmer than many of today's mascots, Wayne the Wizard is outfitted with a navy blue wizard suit adorned with silver stars and moons. His flowing white beard may lead one to classify the mascot as a geezer, but don't be fooled. Wayne can dance and move with the most youthful of fans, which he proves on top of the visiting team's dugout in this photograph taken between innings. (Courtesy of the Fort Wayne Wizards.)

During his years as a professional baseball player, Jim Dwyer played in the minor leagues, the World Series, and everywhere in between. Retiring in 1990, he played for six teams during a career that took him to both leagues, highlighting it as a member of the Baltimore Orioles with a walk-off home run against the Milwaukee Brewers to help his team clinch the 1983 American League East pennant. He then homered in his first World Series at bat against Philadelphia's John Denney. Following his playing career, Dwyer joined the Kenosha Twins as their manager in 1992, becoming their last manager and the Fort Wayne Wizards' first manager the following year in 1993. During his two seasons as the Wizards' manager, his teams posted a 134-140 overall record. (Courtesy of the Fort Wayne Wizards.)

Wayne the Wizard stands ready at the opening gates to welcome fans to the Castle. One such young fan is wearing a pointed wizard hat and suit in Wayne's likeness, a sure hit with the mascot, who stops to pose for the photograph. (Courtesy of the Fort Wayne Wizards.)

Mike Tatoian was the general manager of the Fort Wayne Wizards, who were then a Minnesota Twins affiliate, from 1993 to 1996. He oversaw the development of the new franchise and the development of a new stadium from the ground up. During his tenure, the Wizards set league attendance marks and hosted an exhibition game with the Minnesota Twins, which notably marked the first time in Twins history that the major-league club had visited a Single-A affiliate for a game. (Courtesy of the Fort Wayne Wizards.)

Cleatus Davidson was drafted by the Minnesota Twins in the second round of the 1994 Major League Baseball draft. He played in Fort Wayne with the Wizards in 1997 and was a well-known base stealer as well as an acrobatic defensive second baseman. During that season, Davidson posted 39 stolen bases and eight triples. At the time, he was considered the 12th-best prospect within the Twins organization by *Baseball America*. He was named to the Midwest League All-Star Game alongside Kasey Richardson and starters Chad Moeller and Luis Rivas. In 1999, Davidson was called up to the Twins, where he played in 12 games and had three runs on three hits with two stolen bases in 22 at bats. (Courtesy of the Fort Wayne Wizards.)

Shown here is a mound conference between a Wizards manager and his pitching battery of the day. It is certainly one from the earlier years of the Wizards team as evidenced by the uniform style and design that was worn in the early to mid-1990s. During meetings like this, while the manager and his pitching battery plan how to attack the batter, the Wizards' public address announcer will keep fans in the game with special music or announcements. (Courtesy of the Fort Wayne Wizards.)

Hailing from La Guaira, Venezuela, shortstop Luis Rivas was signed by the Minnesota Twins as an undrafted free agent in 1995. He played in Fort Wayne with the Wizards in 1997 and was considered the No. 1 prospect of the Twins organization at the time. He was named as a starter on the Midwest League All-Star team and earned the league's Best Defensive Shortstop and Infield Arm Awards for the season. He was called up to play with the Twins in 2000 and played a total of 565 games with them over six seasons. In January 2006, he signed with the Tampa Bay Devil Rays. (Courtesy of the Fort Wayne Wizards.)

Michael Cuddyer was a first-round draft choice of the Minnesota Twins in 1997, going ninth overall. During 1998, he compiled an outstanding season with the Wizards by batting .276 with 82 runs and slugging a team-best 12 home runs. He also had 81 RBIs and 16 stolen bases. *Baseball America* considered him to be the Twins' top prospect, and he was also selected to represent the Wizards at the Midwest League All-Star Game that year. He joined the Twins at the major-league level in 2000 and has continued to remain within the organization. (Courtesy of the Fort Wayne Wizards.)

Starting pitcher Brad Thomas signed with the Los Angeles Dodgers in 1995 as an amateur free agent and later signed with the Twins organization after his release. He played with the Wizards in Fort Wayne during the 1998 season and was selected to represent the team at the Midwest League All-Star Game that year. Thomas threw 152 innings, which included a complete game, and 125 strikeouts, and compiled a 2.95 ERA while posting 11 wins. He played parts of three seasons with the Twins beginning in 2001. In 2004, his contact was purchased by the Boston Red Sox and was granted free agency the following October. (Courtesy of the Fort Wayne Wizards.)

In this undated photograph, the Wizards' manager holds an impromptu meeting with his infield during a game. It is the perfect opportunity for the Wizards' public address announcer to tell the fans in attendance what vehicle has been declared the dirtiest vehicle in the parking lot, call out a "celebrity" fan in attendance, or announce the winner of baseball bingo. (Courtesy of the Fort Wayne Wizards.)

Three unidentified Wizards players sit together on the bull pen bench prior to game time. They are probably listening to the blaring music, watching fans arrive, and wondering what the game action will bring. (Courtesy of the Fort Wayne Wizards.)

Both of these photographs are representative of the Wizards as they congratulate one another following separate baseball games at the Castle. Such displays of sportsmanship are common sights to fans who visit the Castle. But the conclusion of Wizards games does not mean the end of the fun and entertainment. For some, it is just the beginning. Young Fort Wayne fans are invited to join together and run the bases, play "launch-a-ball" to win prizes, and more. (Courtesy of the Fort Wayne Wizards.)

Signed by the Padres in 1999 as a free agent, J. J. Trujillo (right) is shown as he is presented with an award at the Castle. During the 2000 season, he thrilled fans in attendance with his submariner delivery as he pursued the Midwest League single-season saves record, ending the season with 42. Despite his minor-league success, he appeared in only four games with the Padres, taking a loss and no wins over 2.7 innings. In March 2004, he was acquired by the Kansas City Royals. (Courtesy of the Fort Wayne Wizards.)

Canadian-born Eric Cyr was a 30th-round selection in the 1998 Major League Baseball draft. He played in five games with the Padres in 2002, going 0-1 in six innings. Cyr was selected off waivers by the Anaheim Angels in March 2003, then by the Cincinnati Reds the following April only to be returned to the Angels in May. In 2004, he was part of the Canadian Summer Olympic team and was on the 2006 Canadian World Baseball Classic roster but chose to sign with the Chinese Professional Baseball League's Uni-President Lions in Taiwan before play in the World Baseball Classic began. As a Wizards player, Cyr threw in 32.2 innings over nine games, posting a 2-2 record and a 4.68 ERA. (Courtesy of the Fort Wayne Wizards.)

Fernando Valenzuela Jr., son of the legendary Dodgers left-hander, is one of several second-generation professional baseball players to spend time at Memorial Stadium as a Fort Wayne Wizards player. Valenzuela played first base and was slotted as a designated hitter during his Wizards tenure. Selected in the 10th round in the 2003 Major League Baseball draft, he spent the entire season in Fort Wayne, batting .295 while going 148 for 502 with 23 doubles, 2 triples, 11 home runs, and 81 RBIs over 135 games. His achievements on the field earned him a selection to the Midwest League All-Star team. (Author's collection.)

Shown here, Fernando Valenzuela Jr. leads off first base. It was a common sight at the Castle during the 2004 campaign. The young first baseman and designated hitter paced the Wizards with 148 hits. (Author's collection.)

Scott Hemmings was selected by the San Diego Padres in the 1997 Major League Baseball draft in the 18th round (560th overall). He joined the Wizards in 1999 at the age of 22 and compiled a moderate .111 batting average over 12 games and 36 at bats. He is seen here before taking one of those attempts at the plate. (Courtesy of the Fort Wayne Wizards.)

Matt Bush was selected first overall in the 2004 draft by the San Diego Padres. The decision to take Bush over other highly rated prospects, like Stephen Drew and Jered Weaver, produced criticism from many observers and made the pick one of controversy. However, the Padres selected Bush knowing they would be able to sign the prospect rather than enter into extensive salary negotiations. At Mission Bay High School, he hit .450 with 11 homers and 35 RBIs during his senior season in addition to an impressive pitching record (9-1 with a 0.42 ERA). He had committed to play for former San Diego Padres great Tony Gwynn at San Diego State University before he was selected in the draft. After taking the field in Peoria and Eugene, Bush joined the Wizards, where he hit .221 and struggled defensively at shortstop. Following an injury at high Single A, Bush returned to the Wizards late in the 2006 season, but his return was cut short due to lingering hamstring troubles. (Author's collection.)

Catcher Colt Morton served three stints with the Fort Wayne Wizards, 22 games in 2003, 36 in 2006, and 63 in 2005, before being promoted to High-A Lake Elsinore. During those 63 games in 2005, Morton provided plenty of offense. In 222 at bats, Morton hit 10 home runs, 46 RBIs, and drew 35 walks. He was named the Midwest League Batter of the Week, for the week ending April 24. During that time, Morton was 7 for 17 with a .412 batting average and a pair of home runs, three runs scored, and six RBIs. Morton was a third-round draft pick by the Padres in the 2003 Major League Baseball draft. He became the first Fort Wayne Wizards player to be named a Midwest League Player of the Week since August 2003 and the first offensive player for the Wizards to earn the Batter of the Week award since May 2003. (Author's collection.)

During the 2005 season, Australian-born Lachlan Dale played in 89 games for the Wizards, collecting 41 runs and 62 hits over 328 at bats. He slugged 12 home runs and hit in 37 base runners. In 2005, Dale was granted his release from the Padres organization. (Author's collection.)

Bryan Edwards delivers a pitch from the mound at the Castle during the 2003 season. The Cincinnati Reds drafted Edwards in the 9th round (273rd overall) of the 2000 amateur entry draft after he played at Northwest Texas Community College. After being released from the Reds in 2002, Edwards signed with the Padres. As a Wizard, Edwards posted a 4-7 record with a 2.40 ERA over 39 games. He began 2006 playing in the New York Mets system, which selected him in the minor-league phase of the Rule V Draft in 2003. (Author's collection.)

The San Diego Padres selected catcher Nick Hundley 76th overall in round two of the 2005 Major League Baseball draft out of the University of Arizona. Going into the draft, Hundley was ranked as one of the top five catchers in the draft. Hundley went 8 for 36 in 10 games with Fort Wayne to end the 2005 season. He returned for the 2006 season, where he hit .274 with 19 doubles, 8 home runs, 44 RBIs, and 29 runs scored in 57 games. The Midwest League selected him as Offensive Player of the Week for the week of June 12–June 18. Hundley was selected to play in the 2006 Midwest League All-Star Game, representing the Fort Wayne Wizards. The following July, he was promoted to High-A Lake Elsinore. (Author's collection.)

On June 13, 2000, Nick Hundley extended his then consecutive game hitting streak to seven games by going three for three with two homers and all three Wizard RBIs. It marked the first multi–home run game for Hundley as a professional. It was one of many highlights during an amazing six-game stretch that included four homers and a 10-for-24 performance that included RBIs in five of the six games. That night, Hundley also threw out both Cedar Rapids runners who attempted to steal bases on him. It was no surprise to most observers when he was selected as the Midwest League Offensive Player of the Week for that time span. (Author's collection.)

Left-handed pitcher Brandon Higelin was selected in the 28th round of the 2005 Major League Baseball draft by the Padres out of California State University, Los Angeles. Having been a late-round selection and putting up average numbers the year before, Higelin did not arrive in Fort Wayne with enormous expectations. However, after modifying his mechanics and working on his two-seam fastball, he posted spectacular numbers as a middle reliever. Through June 28, his hits-to-innings-pitched ratio was 32 to 40.1, and his strikeouts-to-walks ratio was 39 to 12. The result was a selection to represent the Wizards on the 2006 Midwest League All-Star team. (Author's collection.)

Following a successful career at the University of Texas, where his team went to the College World Series four consecutive years, infielder Seth Johnston was taken in the fifth round of the 2005 Major League Baseball draft by the San Diego Padres. Shown here, he receives hitting instructions from the Wizards' third-base coach. Through August 21, he had produced 111 hits over 102 games, which included 30 doubles and 10 home runs. He was selected as a Wizards representative to start the 2006 Midwest League All-Star team. (Author's collection.)

First baseman and designated hitter Daryl Jones was selected by the Padres in the fourth round of the 2004 Major League Baseball draft. Jones was named to the Midwest League All-Star team in 2006, representing the Fort Wayne Wizards. During the third inning of that game, Jones and his Wizards teammate Kyle Blanks delivered back-to-back run-scoring singles to spark a three-run rally with two outs, which snapped a 1-1 tie and helped produce a 7-1 victory. In 2006, he collected 107 hits, 12 home runs, 58 RBIs, and 46 bases on balls over 121 games with the Wizards. Shown here, Jones steps away from first base after a pickoff attempt (above), and he stands ready on offense at the other corner of the field hoping for the opportunity to head home. (Author's collection.)

One of the most exciting players of the Fort Wayne Wizards' 2006 campaign was Will Venable. The son of Fort Wayne Wizards coach (and former big-leaguer) Max Venable, Will was selected by the Padres in the seventh round of the 2005 Major League Baseball draft after performing as a two-sport athlete at Princeton (where he was part of a basketball team that went deep into the NCAA tournament). The left fielder became the second Wizards player of that season to be selected as the Midwest League Offensive Player of the Week, for the week of August 14–20. During that stretch, Venable hit .464 (13 for 28). He also hit 4 home runs, drove in 14 runs, and scored 8 times in a week that saw him produce a .929 slugging percentage capped with a grand slam against the rival South Bend Silverhawks. (Author's collection.)

Kyle Blanks was selected in the 42nd round of the 2004 Major League Baseball draft. He signed days before the 2005 draft after playing a season at a junior college. A towering presence at 6 feet 6 inches and 280 pounds, Blanks is an imposing figure in the batter's box. The 2006 season saw Blanks produce a slugging onslaught, earning a spot on the Midwest League All-Star team and hitting .324 in April. Time at first base and designated hitter was split throughout the season with the Padres other 19-year-old prospect, Daryl Jones, who was also an all-star selection. (Author's collection.)

Kyle Blanks has been pegged with many nicknames because of his size. Names like "Big Nasty" and "Gigantor" have playfully been used by teammates and coaches in reference to Blanks. Despite his large frame, he proved to be a good runner and to be solid defensively. He came to the Wizards rated by *Baseball America* as the best power hitter in the entire Padres farm system. The numbers he produced in Fort Wayne were impressive, especially considering he was forced to miss some action due to an ankle injury. Shown here, Blanks awaits hitting instructions from the Wizards' third-base coach (above) and later lurks off second base in preparation to advance (left). (Author's collection.)

Right-handed pitcher Ben Krosschell was selected in the 15th round of the Major League Baseball draft in 2004 by the Padres out of Highlands Ranch High School. As a young prospect, he drew the interest of many scouts because of a powerful fastball that often reached the mid-to-low 90s. Krosschell started 2006 in Fort Wayne with the Wizards but struggled. In four games, Krosschell earned three losses and gave up 22 hits and 16 earned runs with a bloated 8.47 ERA over 17 innings. He was sent down to extended spring training. Pictured here is Krosschell on the mound during one of his Fort Wayne performances. (Author's collection.)

Mascots are a big part of the on-field entertainment at the Castle when the Wizards play. Sometimes the mascots are more than mascots. On nights when Birdzerk appears, fans are treated to outrageous antics that usually come at the expense of players, managers, and umpires. Shown here, Birdzerk (right) dances with an unsuspecting Wizards player. Between innings, Birdzerk performs a variety of skits. In this particular one, he has coerced a Wizards player into dancing with him during warm-up pitches. Little does this player know, his glove will soon end up thrown over the center field fence as the mascot makes his getaway on an all-terrain vehicle. (Courtesy of the Fort Wayne Wizards.)

Beyond the Base Paths

The Fort Wayne Wizards have enjoyed many years of success as the city's link to minor-league baseball. In addition to baseball, the Wizards provide a superior entertainment package that offers enjoyment for the entire family, whether they are baseball fans or otherwise. In addition, the Wizards sponsor countless community initiatives and consistently bring in national acts to raise the entertainment bar. It can be suggested that much of the Wizards' success has been due, at least in part, to their wonderful community outreach during their tenure. Such actions have positioned the organization as more than a local baseball team, but as a community participant. However, this feature is not unique to the Wizards. Baseball in Fort Wayne has historically produced stories, individuals, and facts that extend beyond the base paths—generating national significance and more in the process.

Allen Hamilton (1798–1864) was among the earliest settlers in Fort Wayne and became a contributor to one of the earliest historical references to professional baseball. In 1861, Hamilton donated a section of land for use as a baseball field on the corner of Lewis and Calhoun Streets. Ten years later, in 1871, the field was the site of the first professional baseball game ever played. The Fort Wayne Kekiongas defeated the Cleveland Forest Citys 2-0. Hamilton immigrated from Ireland in 1820. He and his wife, Emeline (Holman) Hamilton, moved to Allen County in 1823, where he became deputy clerk in the U.S. land office. He was later elected to be the first county sheriff (1824–1826), named postmaster of Fort Wayne (1825–1831), and was county auditor, clerk, and recorder (1831–1838). In 1851, Hamilton joined the Indiana Constitutional Convention as a Whig delegate. In 1859, he served in the Indiana State Senate for one term. Until his death in 1864, Hamilton was active in business as president of the Fort Wayne branch of the Indiana State Bank and of the Allen Hamilton National Bank in Fort Wayne. (Courtesy of the Allen County Public Library.)

In 1944, onlooking fans fill the bleachers at Dwenger Park, which once played host to several semiprofessional teams, including the General Electric club, the Kekiongas, the Capeharts, the Lincoln Lifers, the Dairymen, and more. The park also served as pit stop for several major-league teams (such as the Boston Braves, St. Louis Browns, Philadelphia Phillies, Washington Senators, Cincinnati Reds, and Chicago White Sox) to play against locals in exhibition play. Designed by former major-leaguer and New Haven native William "Pinky" Hargrave, it was considered by many to be one of the best ballparks in the country during its time. (Courtesy of Don Graham.)

Bob Parker personified baseball in Fort Wayne during his time, and no true account of the city and its love affair with the game would be complete without his mention. In addition to being a great baseball liaison to the community, he was well known for his sketches of nationally and locally famous baseball personalities that typically included facts and interesting tidbits of information about the subject. Depicted here is a sketch of Red Carrington, who was another great local ambassador of the game (and a local mailman). In 1967, *Old Fort News* released *Batter Up: Fort Wayne's Baseball History*, which is a compilation of eight Bob Parker installments that originally appeared in the *Fort Wayne Journal-Gazette* in 1957. Through Parker's firsthand accounts of the local history, a great portion of it was preserved for future generations to learn and appreciate. (Courtesy of the Northeast Indiana Baseball Association.)

Louis C. Heilbroner was the founder of Heilbroner's Baseball Bureau Service and the publisher of an annual baseball blue book of statistics, classifications, rules, and schedules that covered the major and minor leagues as well as colleges. He was a scout for the Cincinnati Reds and also served as a manager of the St. Louis Cardinals. Heilbroner also served as president of the Central League for several years and eventually was the lead party in acquiring the Fort Wayne Central League team when Claude Varnell chose to sell the club. The *Chicago Tribune*, reporting on a meeting of Central League owners, showed the level of respect that Heilbroner attained through his contributions when it stated that "prominent baseball men were in attendance, among them being Louis C. Heilbroner of Cincinnati and Fort Wayne without whom no baseball meeting would be complete." (Courtesy of the Library of Congress, Prints and Photographs Division, LC-B2-1409-14.)

The Aveline Hotel stood on the southeast corner of Berry and Calhoun Streets. The six-story complex began construction in 1852, took several years to complete, and was considered a primary business center. In 1908, defective wiring sparked a fire near the elevator shaft on the first floor, and the fire spread throughout the building. Among the guests were Fort Wayne Central League club owner Claude Varnell and his sister, as well as club manager Jack Hendricks, his wife, and their five-year-old son. As the *Sporting News* reported, "Hendricks, with his wife and son were descending the fire escape when the fire broke out below them on the third floor. He swung Mrs. Hendricks over the railing and she dropped to the floor below. Then, he dropped his son over." The fire destroyed the hotel and killed several people, but the Varnells and Hendrickses escaped safely. Shown in the image above is the Aveline Hotel from a postcard during its glory days. The image below shows the hotel from a similar vantage while firefighters attempt to control the blaze. (Above, author's collection; below, courtesy of the Allen County Public Library.)

Known to many as the "baseball evangelist," Billy Sunday began his baseball playing career in 1883 as a member of the Chicago White Stockings, where he promptly struck out in his first 13 at bats. In 1888, he was traded to the Pittsburgh Pirates, where he set a stolen base record of 90 stolen bases in 116 games. He played the sport professionally for eight years, giving it up in 1891 to begin life as a street minister, becoming among the first preachers in the country to make extensive use of the emerging radio medium. Sunday made his home and headquarters near Fort Wayne at Winona Lake from 1911 until his death in 1935. The home has since been restored to its condition of that era with many of the family's original furnishings and is now a Billy Sunday museum that is the centerpiece of many old-time baseball-related events in addition to historical attractions and exhibits. (Courtesy of the Library of Congress, Prints and Photographs Division, LC-B2-1222-15.)

Often considered to be the "Mr. Baseball" of Fort Wayne, Red Carrington was an active participant in anything related to baseball. In 1933, he served as secretary for a young Fort Wayne Amateur Baseball Federation and became president soon afterward. It was a post he would not relinquish for 60 years. In addition, Carrington served as a scout for many Major League Baseball teams and as president of the North American Baseball Federation and Fort Wayne's Baseball and Softball Commission. He was inducted into the local baseball hall of fame in 1967 and the East Chicago hall of fame in 1983. In 1978, the old utilities park in Fort Wayne was renamed Carrington Field in his honor. The field was later relocated in the early 1990s when the Fort Wayne Wizards came to the community and Memorial Stadium was built on the same grounds. The field is to be relocated again in 2007, following the site owner's decision to develop the land for other uses. (Courtesy of the Northeast Indiana Baseball Association.)

On January 20, 1955, Dodger great Jackie Robinson paid visit to Fort Wayne for a special "Meet Jackie Robinson" event that was held at the Central Catholic High School. Shown in the photograph above are some of Fort Wayne's more prominent baseball leaders with Robinson. From left to right are Red Carrington, Vern Krauss, Robinson, Carl Gunkler, and John "Red" Braden. Shown below is a ticket that permitted entrance to the highly attended event. (Above, courtesy of the Northeast Indiana Baseball Association; below, courtesy of Don Graham.)

"Meet Jackie Robinson"

CENTRAL CATHOLIC HIGH SCHOOL

130 East Lewis

THURSDAY, JANUARY 20, 1955

2:00 P.M. (Doors Open 1:30)

• Limited to Seating Capacity Only •

Memorial Stadium greets many early arriving fans as they enter the gates. Each year, new Fort Wayne Wizards players are selected to have their image adorn the front facade of the Castle, where "amazing baseball" happens on the field. This picture also appears on the back cover of the book. (Courtesy of the Fort Wayne Wizards.)

Many young fans take in the action on the field while watching Wizards pitchers warm up along the right field foul line. The spacious seating from the ballpark deck provides comfortable, close-up access to the players as well as an excellent view of the action—plus, it is a great spot to snag a foul ball or two. (Courtesy of the Fort Wayne Wizards.)

This unique photograph provides a view of the action from the players' point of view in the home dugout along first base. A Wizards player is up to bat as another Wizards player stands ready in the on-deck circle. Meanwhile their teammates station themselves to be ready if a foul ball races into the dugout. (Courtesy of the Fort Wayne Wizards.)

This photograph of a Wizards helmet and promotional ball presents an excellent view of the Fort Wayne Wizards logo. Through the first 13 years of the Wizards' history, the logo was always two letters. Prior to the 2006 season, the Wizards introduced an alternate logo, which was the first single-letter logo in the team's history. The "Magic W" consists of an uppercase *W* with a baseball wrapping around it with a "magic" trail of moons and stars. It also incorporates a new lighter blue color that replaced a green highlight from previous logos. (Courtesy of the Fort Wayne Wizards.)

Each year, the Fort Wayne Wizards and Huntington University partner to host a Christian speaker series. The invited speakers discuss their faith as Christians and the impact it has had throughout their lives during a postgame testimonial. One of the first speakers to visit the Castle to share their experiences with Fort Wayne fans was Dave Dravecky, who was a major-league pitcher until he lost an arm through amputation due to cancer. He shared a heartfelt and inspirational story of overcoming life's challenges and maintaining faith while doing so. Pictured here are two photographs taken during Dravecky's visit. (Courtesy of the Fort Wayne Wizards.)

An unidentified Harry Carey impersonator poses with an imitation WGN microphone and oversize black-rimmed novelty glasses in front of the grandstands at the Castle—just outside the broadcast booth. On occasion, fans are treated to an inning or two done in a style and manner eerily reminiscent of the broadcasting legend. (Courtesy of the Fort Wayne Wizards.)

The number of individuals who have participated in the singing of the national anthem during pregame activities at the Castle is countless. Individuals, groups, and organizations are invited to perform their renditions as fans turn their attention to the American flag in center field. Shown here, an unidentified group of individuals performs prior to the game as fans—and mascots—pay their respects. (Courtesy of the Fort Wayne Wizards.)

In July 2001, James Earl Jones paid a special visit to Fort Wayne. Part of that visit entailed taking time out to share the joy of reading with some of the Wizards' youngest fans. Above, Jones appears with several members of the Wizards' front office staff, including general manager Mike Nutter, who is standing second from left. Below, Jones reads the Ernest Lawrence Thayer classic *Casey at the Bat* to "Reading Champions" who were nominated from more than 80,000 participants. Jones later read the national anthem over the Memorial Stadium speaker system, finishing by roaring "Play ball!" so loudly it shook the crowd of nearly 6,200. (Courtesy of the Fort Wayne Wizards.)

When General Sports and Entertainment of Rochester, Michigan, purchased the Fort Wayne Wizards in 1999, it brought with it a new mascot: a dragon. A public contest was held throughout the community for entrants to select the name of the new mascot. Of the entrants, the organization selected the name Dinger the Dragon. Since Dinger's arrival, it has given Wayne the Wizard a little less time in the spotlight as Dinger's face and likeness appear on most promotional materials. However, they both insist that no animosity exists between the duo. Pictured here, Dinger the Dragon and Wayne the Wizard share a good book. (Courtesy of the Fort Wayne Wizards.)

In addition to thousands of fans annually, the Castle is often frequented by local and national celebrities. And sometimes, one might even see the most unlikely of guests. Pictured here is a certain mascot that must have gotten lost during one of his team's road trips. (Courtesy of the Fort Wayne Wizards.)

Dinger's likeness appears on many of the promotional and giveaway items. Pictured is senior assistant general manager David Lorenz, donning a Dinger foam hat as he prepares to hand out Wizards pennants to fans as they enter the Castle. (Courtesy of the Fort Wayne Wizards.)

Local organizations often partner with the Fort Wayne Wizards to sponsor the giveaway night. Shown here, Wizards employees hand out Wizards sweatshirts with a cosponsoring company's logo on the back side. (Courtesy of the Fort Wayne Wizards.)

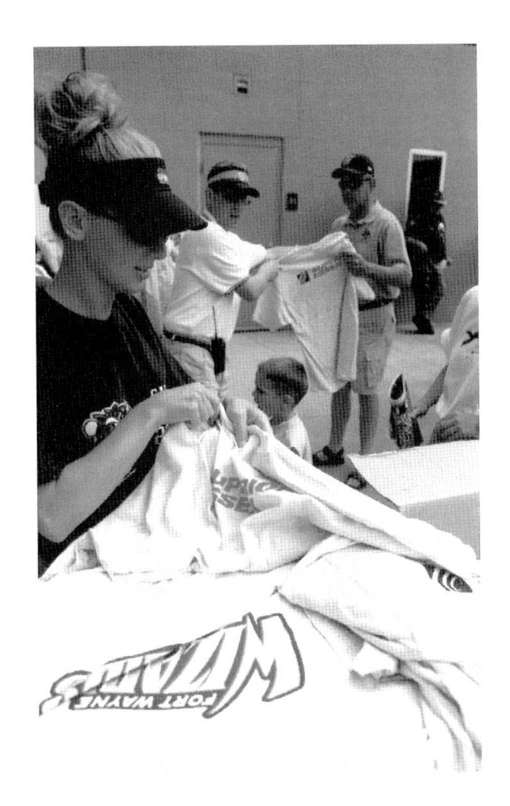

One of the popular giveaway promotions at the Castle is baseball bat giveaway day. Often fans who attend and receive a bat will ask Wizards players and coaches (and Dinger) to sign their bat for a unique souvenir. And if one does not get to the park in time for the giveaway, cracked and broken bats that were actually used by Wizards players during games and batting practice can be purchased inside the team store. (Courtesy of the Fort Wayne Wizards.)

Upon entering the front gates, every fan is greeted by a Wizards employee and offered a souvenir program with information and articles about the team, players, and more. They also make wonderful items for fans to obtain player autographs. (Courtesy of the Fort Wayne Wizards.)

Before the game, fans make sure they get their baseball bingo cards to play along throughout the game. Based upon the plays that occur on the field, numbers appear on the scoreboard. Fans who return completed bingo cards receive prizes, including gift certificates, car washes, and more. (Courtesy of the Fort Wayne Wizards.)

Before the game begins, Dinger can often be found on the main concourse meeting and greeting fans. The younger fans flock to the dragon, who is more than happy to say hello and thank them for their support of the team. (Courtesy of the Fort Wayne Wizards.)

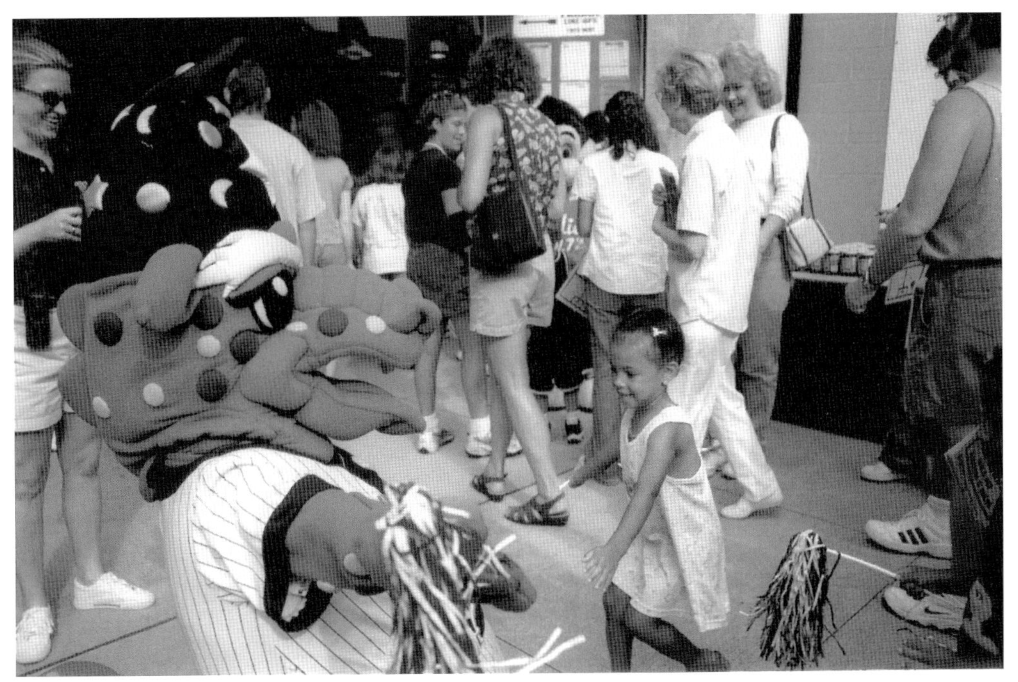

Dinger the Dragon greets a young fan who is excited to meet him. Meanwhile other fans take a moment to meet with another mascot in the background. (Courtesy of the Fort Wayne Wizards.)

Water bottles line a table before a game as they wait to become giveaway items for fans who will be attending. The giveaway, cosponsored by Juicy Juice and the Wizards, is sure to provide welcome relief from the heat that pours into Memorial Stadium during July and August. (Courtesy of the Fort Wayne Wizards.)

An unidentified Wizards player stands near home plate prior to game time clutching a baseball bat. Surely he is surveying the field, the bases, and the mound while envisioning the upcoming contest. In the background, two members of the umpire crew discuss their roles and responsibilities in calling the upcoming game. (Courtesy of the Fort Wayne Wizards.)

Major Connections

Since the Wizards have been located in Fort Wayne, they have been affiliated as a Single-A minor-league baseball franchise, first with the Minnesota Twins and later with the San Diego Padres. Under the umbrella of both parent organizations, Fort Wayne has had the privilege of watching more than 50 players journey through the city who have gone on to play on Major League Baseball clubs. Countless others have come through the city as opponents of the Wizards. While some of the Wizards players appear to be sure things to make it to the grandest stage, such as No. 1 draft selections, that is not always the way it works out. Meanwhile some players are talents who rise through the developmental ranks to the surprise of many onlookers. During their tenure, the Wizards have had some first-round draft choices, such as Sean Burroughs, Dan Serafini, and Matt LeCroy, who have gone on to play in the major leagues. From the first-year Wizards in 1993, five players made it, and many others have since joined them. What follows in this concluding chapter is the city's and the Wizards' connection to Major League Baseball player development.

Among the most successful and well-known Fort Wayne Wizards is Torii Hunter, who has gone on to play many years on the major-league level with the Minnesota Twins. Through the 2006 season, Hunter has played his entire career within the Twins organization. In the spring of 1993, Hunter was selected in the first round of the Major League Baseball draft, going 20th overall. He joined the Wizards for the 1994 season, which was the team's second year in Fort Wayne. Hunter turned in a solid .293 average with the Wizards that year and played center field masterfully under the direction of manager Jim Dwyer. He also posted 10 home runs and 50 RBIs, scoring 57 runs in 91 games with the team. (Courtesy of the Fort Wayne Wizards.)

Before he was turning heads with dazzling plays in the Metrodome on the major-league level, Torii Hunter was polishing and fine-tuning his act at the Castle in Fort Wayne. Shown here, Hunter makes a spectacular leap against signage on the outfield wall to rob an opposing batter of what would have been a sure extra-base hit. (Courtesy of the Fort Wayne Wizards.)

Torii Hunter takes batting practice as a member of the Fort Wayne Wizards. When he took part in his first spring training, the Twins organization strategically placed Hunter's locker between the lockers of Twins legends Kirby Puckett and Dave Winfield. Without a doubt, the tactic worked out well for the team and Hunter. (Courtesy of the Fort Wayne Wizards.)

In another photograph of Torii Hunter taking batting practice, he displays his hitting skills. Since leaving the Wizards, Hunter has taken an initiative in developing programs to help inner-city children have the opportunity to learn and play baseball. (Courtesy of the Fort Wayne Wizards.)

In 1992, the Minnesota Twins drafted right-handed pitcher Dan Naulty in the 14th round of the Major League Baseball draft. He appeared in 97 games with the Twins on the major-league level between 1996 and 1998, compiling a 4-5 record over 111.4 innings. He was traded to the New York Yankees in 1998 in exchange for minor-leaguer Allen Butler. In 1999, the Los Angeles Dodgers acquired Naulty from the Yankees for minor-league first baseman Nicholas Leach. (Courtesy of the Fort Wayne Wizards.)

In 1993, LaTroy Hawkins put together what is arguably the best single-season performance of any Fort Wayne Wizards pitcher. His 2.06 ERA, 15-5 record, and 179 strikeouts are indicative of the many awards and records he obtained that season. Entering the 2006 campaign, Hawkins still maintained Wizards records in ERA (2.06), wins (15), complete games (4), shutouts (2), strikeouts in a season (179), and strikeouts in a game (15). Even more impressive is that Hawkins accomplished these totals during the inaugural season of the Wizards organization and they still stand 13 years later. He broke into the major leagues with the Twins in 1995 and has since also played with the Chicago Cubs, San Francisco Giants, and Baltimore Orioles. (Courtesy of the Fort Wayne Wizards.)

Matt Lawton joined the Fort Wayne Wizards during the club's first season in 1993. He was drafted by the Minnesota Twins in the 13th round of the 1991 Major League Baseball draft. Lawton went on to join the parent club in 1995. A former all-star, he has been primarily a journeyman since 2001, having played with the Twins, Mets, Indians, Cubs, Yankees, Pirates, and Mariners during that time. (Courtesy of the Fort Wayne Wizards.)

Dan Serafini was another component of the talented 1993 Wizards squad that made up the team's first year in the city. He was drafted in the first round (26th overall) in the 1992 Major League Baseball draft. He broke into the big leagues in 1995 with the Twins and was later purchased by the Chicago Cubs in 1999, only to be traded to the San Diego Padres later in the year. Since then, Serafini played in seven other major-league organizations before being granted his release from the Reds in 2003. He concluded his major-league career with a 15-16 record over 101 games and 263.3 innings pitched. (Courtesy of the Fort Wayne Wizards.)

Third baseman Michael Ryan was drafted by the Minnesota Twins in the fifth round of the 1996 Major League Baseball draft. He debuted with the Twins in September 2002 and appeared in 127 games before being granted his release. In 2005, he signed as a free agent with the Atlanta Braves organization. As a member of the Wizards in 1998, he posted the team's highest batting average with .318, was the Twins' Minor League Player of the Month for May, and was a selection to the Midwest League All-Star team. (Courtesy of the Fort Wayne Wizards.)

Third baseman Corey Koskie joined the Fort Wayne Wizards for the 1995 season. He was a 26th-round draft selection of the Minnesota Twins in 1994, making his debut with the big-league club in 1998. He continued to play with the Twins through 2004 when he signed with the Toronto Blue Jays before the 2005 season. After one year with the Blue Jays, he was traded to the Milwaukee Brewers. With Fort Wayne, he appeared in 123 games, posting a .310 batting average with 143 hits, 78 RBIs, and 16 home runs. (Courtesy of the Fort Wayne Wizards.)

Catcher A. J. Pierzynski was selected in the third round (71st overall) by the Minnesota Twins in the 1994 draft. He joined the Wizards for 22 games in 1995 and 114 in 1996. In 515 at bats, Pierzynski collected 144 hits, 35 doubles, and 84 RBIs. He debuted with the Twins in 1998 and remained with the organization until being traded to the San Francisco Giants in return for Boof Bonzer, Joe Nathan, and Francisco Liriano in 2003. After being released by the Giants, he signed with the White Sox in 2004 and went on to claim a World Series ring in 2005. The following year, he ran over Chicago Cubs catcher Michael Barrett at home plate on a close play. Pierzynski smacked his hand on home plate and drew the ire of Barrett, who stood and punched Pierzynski in the jaw, inciting a brawl between the teams. (Courtesy of the Fort Wayne Wizards.)

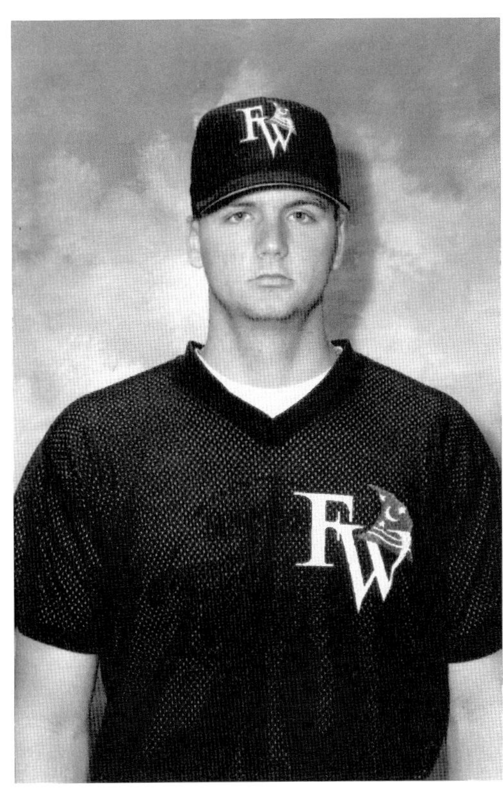

Originally selected in the second round of the 1994 Major League Baseball draft by the New York Mets, Matt LeCroy chose Clemson University over the Mets. He was then drafted in the first round (50th overall) by the Minnesota Twins in the 1997 draft. He joined the Fort Wayne Wizards in 1998 for 64 games and produced 62 hits and 33 runs in 225 at bats. He was a minor-league all-star and Minnesota Twins Minor League Player of the Year in 1999, making his major-league debut the following year. (Courtesy of the Fort Wayne Wizards.)

In 2001, the San Diego Padres, parent club of the Fort Wayne Wizards, paid a visit to the Castle. In addition to making public appearances and signing autographs, Padres players met with Wizards players to share experiences and tutor the young squad. Shown above is Padres starting pitcher Bobby Jones as he takes in the sights of the game and stadium from the bench. Below, a Padres player shares game wisdom with a Fort Wayne Wizards counterpart. (Courtesy of the Fort Wayne Wizards.)

When the San Diego Padres came through Fort Wayne for their exhibition contest against the Wizards, the most well-known name on the club was Tony Gwynn, who was playing in his final major-league season. Although he battled nagging injuries throughout the year and could not play in the game, he took time out to sit down with Wizards players and discuss his experiences and offer advice to the minor-league squad. Shown above, Gwynn talks with an unidentified Wizards player. Below, the Wizards players sit on the edge of their dugout seats as Gwynn talks about the game. (Courtesy of the Fort Wayne Wizards.)

The Wizards players were not the only group of fans interested in meeting with Tony Gwynn when the Padres came to town. Shown above, Gwynn signs autographs and talks with local fans who take advantage of their rare opportunity to take home a souvenir signed by a definite future National Baseball Hall of Fame inductee. (Courtesy of the Fort Wayne Wizards.)

Shown here, players from the Padres team meet with fans along the fence before game time to sign autographs and talk baseball. Although the Wizards did their best to make the game competitive, the parent club defeated its minor-league counterparts during the afternoon game. (Courtesy of the Fort Wayne Wizards.)

Shown above, many Major League Baseball hopefuls meet in the picnic/kids area at the Castle to register for tryouts, hosted by the parent club. Hundreds of dreaming athletes have shown up each time the Padres deployed scouts to Fort Wayne to seek out talent for their minor-league developmental system. Below, a group of would-be minor-leaguers meet in center field and take a few moments to prepare to participate in drills for major-league scouts. (Courtesy of the Fort Wayne Wizards.)

Sean Burroughs was a standout player of the Little League World Series in 1992 and 1993. He was also a member of the gold-medal United States baseball team in 2000 at the Olympics in Sydney, Australia. In 1998, the Padres made Burroughs the 9th overall pick in the Major League Baseball draft. As a Wizards player in 1999, he produced a record .359 batting average, 153 hits, 80 RBIs, and 65 runs over 122 games and 426 at bats. Burroughs also holds the Wizards record for the longest hitting streak (23 games) and most consecutive games of reaching base by walk or hit (56). His play made him a natural selection for the Midwest League All-Star team and being named the San Diego Padres Minor League Player of the Year in 1999. By 2002, he was playing with the parent club. Shown here is Burroughs at bat (right) and on first base prior to a pickoff attempt (below) at PetCo Park in San Diego during his final year with the Padres. He was later traded to the Tampa Bay Devil Rays. (Author's collection.)

Sean Burroughs rose quickly through the Padres' minor-league system. Shown here is Burroughs's profile on the scoreboard at PetCo Park prior to an at bat. He is one of more than 50 former Wizards who have made it to the major leagues. (Author's collection.)

Second baseman Josh Barfield is the son of former major-leaguer Jesse Barfield. He was selected by the San Diego Padres in the fourth round of the 2001 Major League Baseball draft. After a brief stay in Idaho Falls, he joined the Fort Wayne Wizards in 2002 and quickly proved his abilities to teammates and fans. (Courtesy of the Fort Wayne Wizards.)

Barfield poses for a promotional shot (right) and displays his on-field talents at second base (below). During the 2001 season, Barfield compiled a .306 average while producing 164 hits, 73 runs, and 57 RBIs, and swiping 26 bases over 129 games and 536 at bats. Following his tenure with the Wizards, he was named the San Diego Padres Minor League Player of the Year in 2003 and surprised many observers when he won the Padres starting job at second out of spring training in 2006. During that time, he batted .433 with 20 runs and 18 RBIs over 21 games. (Courtesy of the Fort Wayne Wizards.)

Jake Peavy was selected in the 15th round of the 1999 Major League Baseball draft. As a member of the Fort Wayne Wizards in 2000, the 19-year-old Peavy posted a 2.90 ERA and a 13-8 record over 26 games and 133.1 innings pitched. (Courtesy of the Fort Wayne Wizards.)

Following Peavy's tenure with the Fort Wayne Wizards in 2000, the pitcher embarked on a rapid rise through the San Diego Padres' minor-league system. By 2002, he had secured a spot in the parent club's rotation, twice being recognized as the Padres Player of the Year (2004 and 2005). Over his first four major-league seasons, Peavy compiled a 57-45 record with a 3.51 ERA. Shown here are two images of Peavy tossing pitches while in Fort Wayne Wizards attire. (Courtesy of the Fort Wayne Wizards.)

Fort Wayne native Eric Wedge was named the *Sporting News*'s 2002 Minor League Manager of the Year. That same year, he was hired to lead the Cleveland Indians team, effectively becoming the youngest manager in Major League Baseball at 34 years of age. Shown here, Wedge poses next to an Indians jersey, a team photograph, and a Northrop High School jersey during an event held in Fort Wayne. Wedge starred as a catcher for the school's baseball team from 1983 to 1986. As a freshman on the varsity squad, he helped his team secure a state championship in 1983. (Courtesy of the Fort Wayne Sports Corporation.)

Following his playing career, which ended after several surgeries, Wedge began his managerial career in Low-A Columbus. The next year, he won Manager of the Year honors with the High-A team in Kinston, North Carolina. In 2001, he was named the International League (Triple-A) Manager of the Year after leading the Buffalo Bisons. His success has shown his ability to be not only an exceptional student of the game but a teacher as well. Shown in the photograph to the right is Wedge as he speaks in front of a local crowd. The event took place one evening as Wedge was in town to conduct his annual Eric Wedge Baseball Camp. In the photograph below, Wedge instructs area kids on the many aspects of the game. (Courtesy of the Fort Wayne Sports Corporation.)

Eric Wedge (right) stands next to baseball camp director Caleb Kimmel as he prepares to take part in instructing infield drills during Wedge's instructional camp, held in Fort Wayne at the ASH Centre (formerly Tahcumah Sports and Recreation). (Courtesy of the Fort Wayne Sports Corporation.)

Kimmel (right) stands next to Homestead High School friend and teammate Rob Bowen. Kimmel is the owner of Between the Lines, a special events planning company that seeks to make a positive impact on the community and the lives of area youth by providing quality athletic and recreational programs, leadership, and role models. (Courtesy of Rob Bowen, with special thanks to Caleb Kimmel.)

Bowen is a 1999 graduate of Homestead High School and the most recent area native to make it to the major leagues, breaking in with the San Diego Padres in 2006. He was selected by the Minnesota Twins in the second round (56th overall) of the 1999 Major League Baseball draft. He continued to play in the Twins organization until 2006, later acquired by the Padres from waivers. Shown to the right is Bowen in his Homestead High School uniform. Below, Bowen poses while in the Minnesota Twins organization. (Courtesy of Rob Bowen, with special thanks to Caleb Kimmel.)

A vintage Fort Wayne jersey is shown (left) from the author's collection. Having seen countless innings and game action on the field, the jersey serves as a reminder of baseball days gone by as a Wizards pitcher (below) delivers his best stuff to an opposing hitter. Late in the 2006 season, the Wizards were on the verge of a third consecutive playoff berth, several recent high-round draft picks were joining the squad, and outfielder Will Venable was named to the Midwest League Post-Season All-Star team based upon a spectacular season. As a new downtown stadium is discussed and considered, Fort Wayne's baseball heritage and drive for future success are as strong as ever. (Below, courtesy of the Fort Wayne Wizards.)

Throughout the season, fans in attendance are treated to several postgame fireworks displays that are accompanied by choreographed music. Shown here, Wizards mascot and youth liaison Dinger the Dragon and a few young fans share a portion of the infield to get the best view in the Castle as massive and colorful fireworks boom overhead. (Courtesy of the Fort Wayne Wizards.)

BIBLIOGRAPHY

Benson, Michael. *Ballparks of North America: A Comprehensive Historical Reference to Baseball Grounds, Yards and Stadiums 1845 to present.* Jefferson, NC: McFarland and Company, Inc., 1989.

Fort Wayne Wizards Media Guide 2006. Fort Wayne, IN: 2006.

Graham, Don, ed. *Line Drives.* Fort Wayne, IN.

New York Times. New York: 1871.

1992 Kenosha Twins Official Yearbook. Kenosha, WI: 1992.

Parker, Bob. *Batter Up: Fort Wayne's Baseball History.* Fort Wayne, IN: The Allen County–Fort Wayne Historical Society, 1967.

Smith, Ben. "Baseball in Fort Wayne Meant Most to Braden." *Fort Wayne Journal-Gazette.* 2002.

Spalding, Chas H. "The Loss of Claude H. Varnell." *Sporting News.* 1912.

PLAYER INDEX

Consistent with our mission to preserve history on a local level, this book was printed in South Carolina on American-made paper and manufactured entirely in the United States. Products carrying the accredited Forest Stewardship Council (FSC) label are printed on 100 percent FSC-certified paper.